R.E.M. AROUND the sun

WWW.REMHQ.COM

Transcribed by DANNY BEGELMAN
and BILL LaFLEUR

Project Managers: CAROL CUELLAR and AARON STANG
Music Editor: COLGAN BRYAN
Book Art Layout: JANEL HARRISON
Album Art: © 2004 R.E.M./Athens, LLC

CONTENTS

AROUND THE SUN

G
D
F♯m
- low - ers would lead
with a voice
To dream? Be - lieve?
E
G
D
A
so strong it could knock me to my knees.
Give me a voice so strong I can ques - tion what I have seen.
Chorus:
G
Bm
D
E
Hold on, world, 'cause you don't know what's com - ing.
Acous. Gtr.
hold throughout
*Elec. Gtr. 1
mf hold throughout
*Second time only.
G
Bm
D
E
Acous. Gtr. cont. simile
Hold on, world, 'cause I'm not jump - ing off.

G
Bm
D
E
Hold on to__ this boy____ a lit - tle long - er.
1.
C
G
D
D.C.
Take an - oth - er trip____ a - round__ the sun.____
Acous. Gtr.
2.
C
G
Take an - oth - er trip a - round__ the sun.__

Bridge:
D7
213
A - round_ the sun._
Acous. & Elec. Gtr.
hold
hold
hold
A - round_ the sun._
hold
hold
hold
Acous. & Elec. Gtrs. cont. simile
A - round_ the sun.___
A - round_ the sun._
A - round__ the sun.____
Acous. & Elec. Gtr.
hold
hold

(Down)
(hold)
T
A
B
Slower ♩= 72
Outro:
D
Fmaj7
C
Em
G
Acous. Gtr.
Cont. rhy. simile
Let my dreams set me free.
Be - lieve
Be - lieve.
Na na na na na now.
(Na na na now.)
Na na na na na na now.
(Na na na na now.
Na na na na na na now.
)
(Na na na na now. Now.)
Na na na na na now.
(Na na na na na now.)
(Na na na na na now.)

AFTERMATH

Words and Music by
PETER BUCK, MIKE MILLS, MICHAEL STIPE

Chorus:
C
Bb
F
up to you to fix it. Now you've worked it out,
* Elec. Gtr. 2
Rhy. Fig. 1
*Elec. Gtr. 2, 3rd time only.
and you see it all. And you've
end Rhy. Fig. 1
w/Rhy. Fig. 1 (Elec. Gtr. 2) 2 times, 3rd time only
worked it out, and you see it all. And you want to shout
To Coda
1.
Acous. Gtr.
how you see it all. 2. It's

2.
Interlude:
E♭
6fr.
1333
B♭
1333
E♭
6fr.
1333
Acous. Gtr. resume rhy. fig. simile
Elec. Gtr. 2
mf
Elec. Gtr. 1
mf
D.S. 𝄋 al Coda
B♭
1333
Am
231
F
134211
Acous. Gtr.
3. Now the

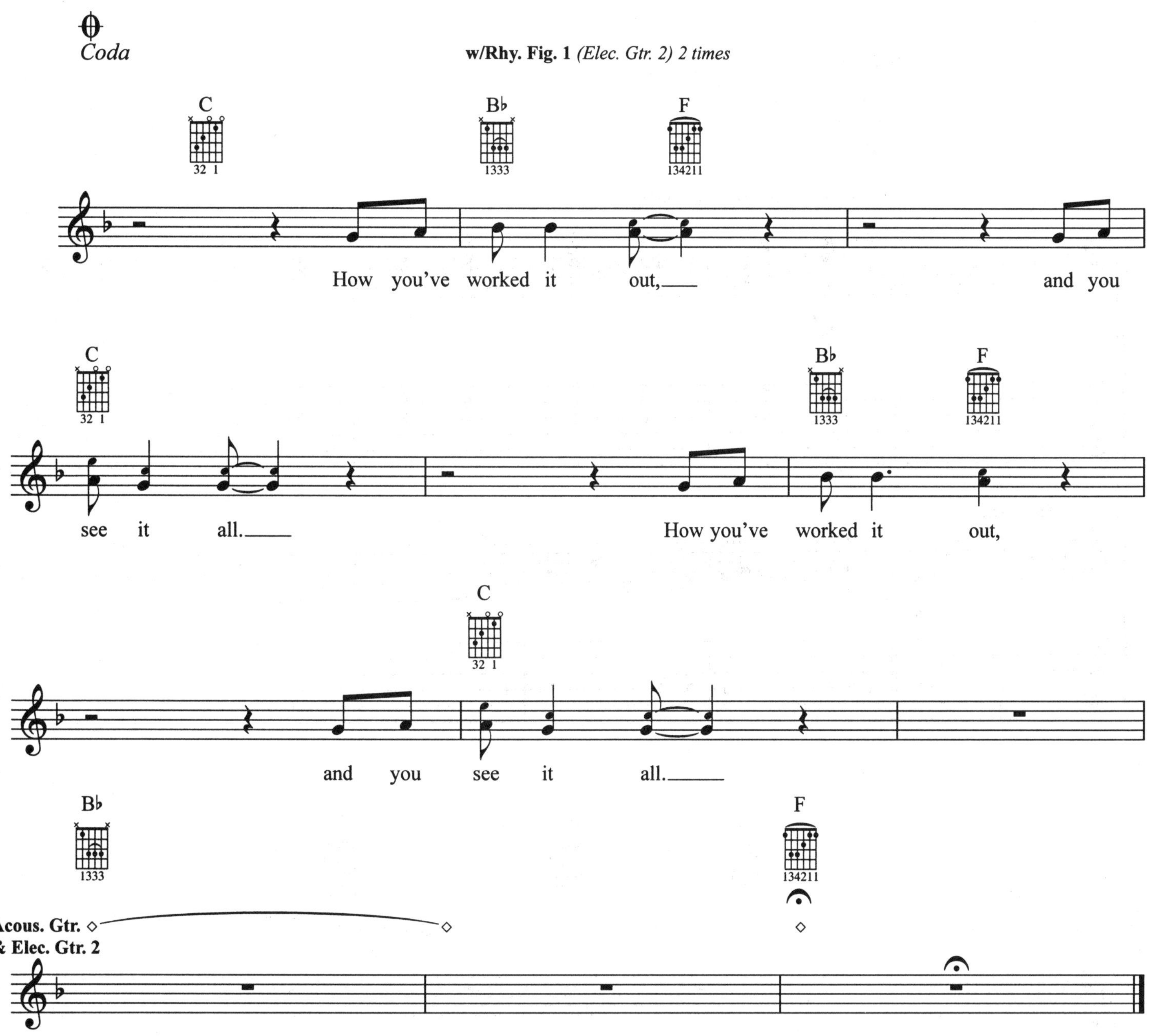

Verse 2:
It's easy to dismiss the "What's it all about" crowd.
There is no doubt. It's this, here, now.
And you close your eyes.
He's not coming back.
So you work it out, overfeed the cat.
And the plants are dry and they need to drink.
So you do your best, and you flood the sink.
Sit down in the kitchen and cry.
(To Chorus:)

Verse 3:
Now the universe left you for a runner's lap.
It feels like home when it comes crashing back.
And it makes you laugh
Anid it makes you cry,
When London falls and you're still alive.
The radio stutters, it makes you laugh
And the aftermath,
Open up your eyes,
You're so alive.
(To Chorus:)

BOY IN THE WELL

Words and Music by
PETER BUCK, MIKE MILLS, MICHAEL STIPE

Em6
D(4)
3fr.
C
know what it's bring - ing on. You might as well say it. I
Em
Em6
D(4)
see it, I feel it, this town is go - ing wrong. It's
Chorus:
C
Am
G
Fsus
F
Elec. Gtr.
turn-ing a - way. You want-ed me to be some-one that I could nev - er be.
Cont. rhy. simile
My new friends are of - fer-ing things I've nev - er dreamed. It's beau-ti-ful. I'd like for them to
To Coda
1.
2.
Bb
Am
take me on. 2. The
Interlude:
D
C
open
Cont. rhy. simile
Synth.

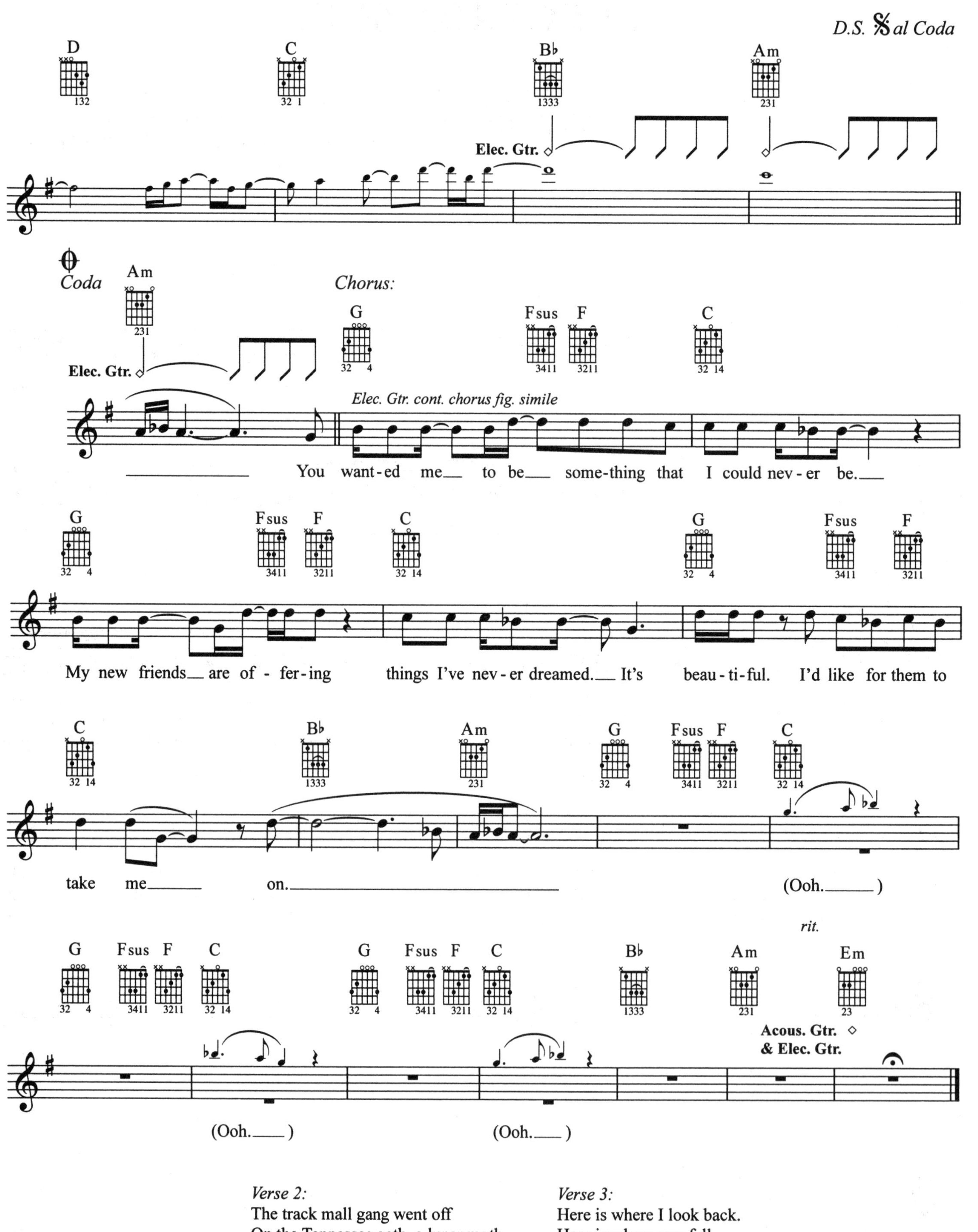

Verse 2:
The track mall gang went off
On the Tennessee goth, a lunar moth,
You chrysalis and flail.
The water is rising. You try to rappel.
A rousing cheer for the boy in the well.
(To Pre-chorus:)

Verse 3:
Here is where I look back.
Here is where you fell.
This is where I got up,
Shaking off my tail.
This is where your rope trick
Started to look stale.
A Greyhound pass for the boy in the well.
(To Pre-chorus:)

ELECTRON BLUE

Suggested guitar chords for Verse

F
Gm/C
8fr.
10fr.
13331
1321

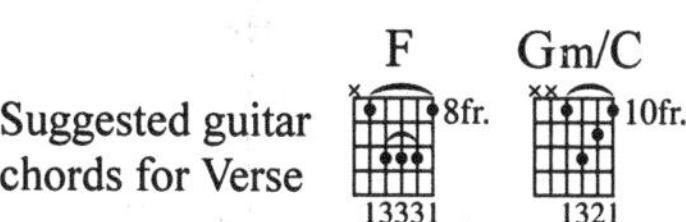

Words and Music by
PETER BUCK, MIKE MILLS, MICHAEL STIPE

Moderately ♩ = 98

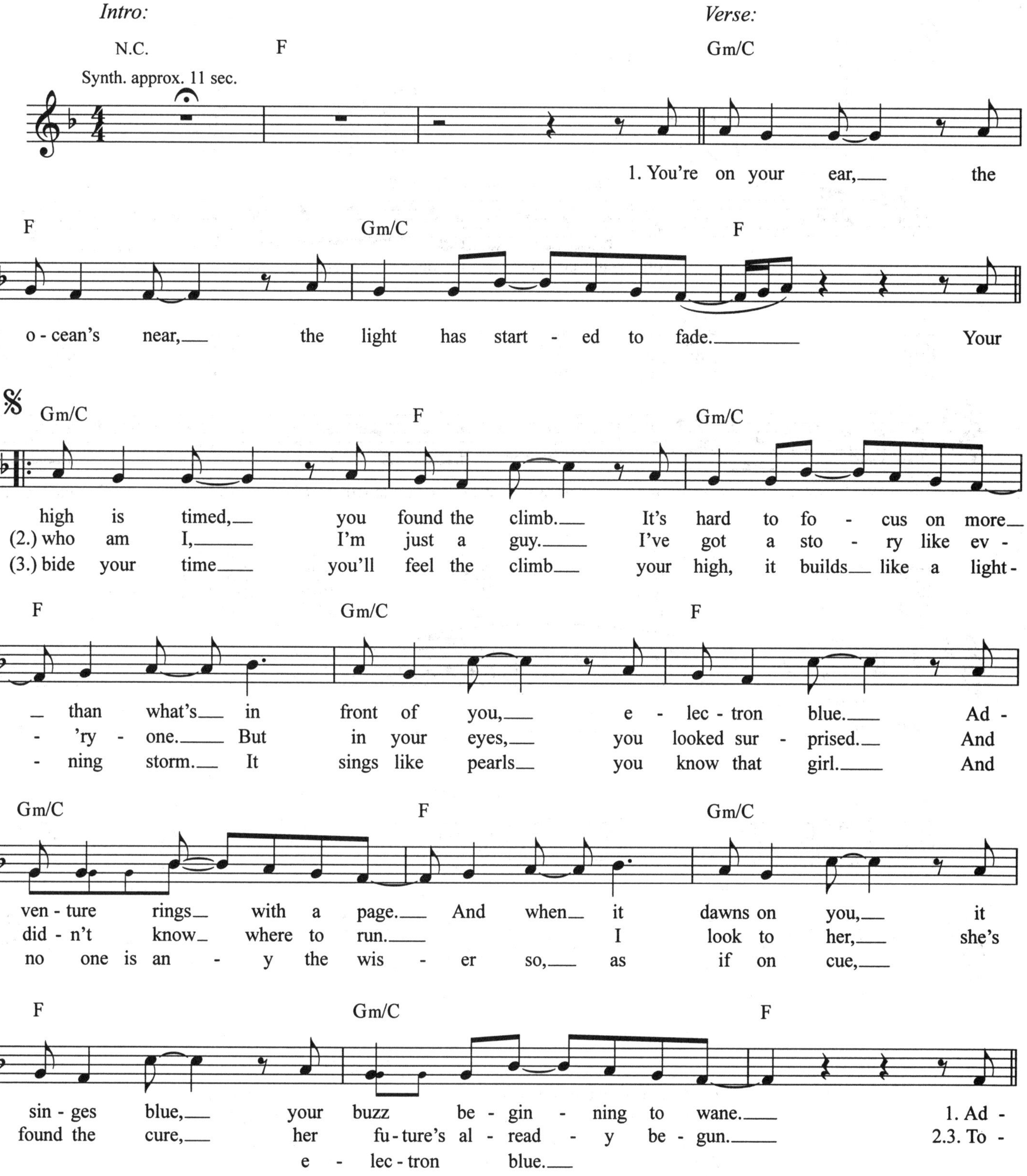

Intro:
N.C.
F
Synth. approx. 11 sec.
Verse:
Gm/C
1. You're on your ear, the
F Gm/C F
o - cean's near, the light has start - ed to fade. Your
Gm/C F Gm/C
high is timed, you found the climb. It's hard to fo - cus on more
(2.) who am I, I'm just a guy. I've got a sto - ry like ev -
(3.) bide your time you'll feel the climb your high, it builds like a light -
F Gm/C F
than what's in front of you, e - lec - tron blue. Ad -
'ry - one. But in your eyes, you looked sur - prised. And
ning storm. It sings like pearls you know that girl. And
Gm/C F Gm/C
ven - ture rings with a page. And when it dawns on you, it
did - n't know where to run. I look to her, she's
no one is an - y the wis - er so, as if on cue,
F Gm/C F
sin - ges blue, your buzz be - gin - ning to wane. 1. Ad -
found the cure, her fu - ture's al - read - y be - gun. 2.3. To -
e - lec - tron blue.

Chorus:
Dm
C
Am
ven - ture has laid its claim on you, it's all you want to do.
mor - row is gain - ing speed on you, it's all you want to do.
Elec. Gtr. Rhy. Fig. 1
mf
w/Rhy. Fig. 1 (Elec. Gtr.)
G
Dm
C
You, you know where to run,
end Rhy. Fig. 1
1.
Am
G
Gm/C
Guitar tacet
you run e - lec - tron blue.
2.3.
F
Gm/C
F
G
2. And - tron blue. You,

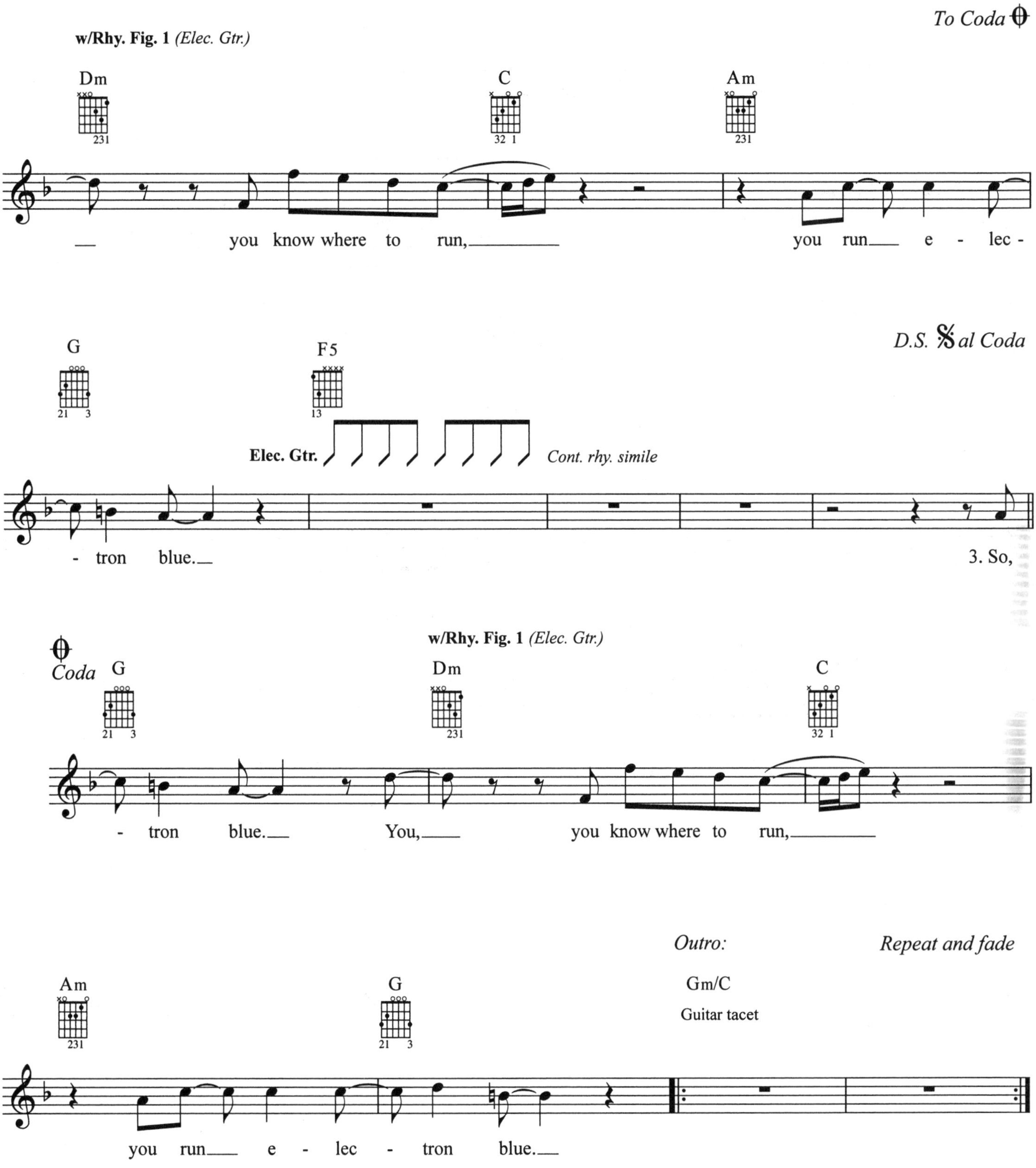

To Coda
w/Rhy. Fig. 1 (Elec. Gtr.)
Dm
C
Am
you know where to run,
you run e - lec -
G
F5
D.S. al Coda
Elec. Gtr.
Cont. rhy. simile
- tron blue.
3. So,
Coda
G
w/Rhy. Fig. 1 (Elec. Gtr.)
Dm
C
- tron blue. You, you know where to run,
Outro:
Repeat and fade
Am
G
Gm/C
Guitar tacet
you run e - lec - tron blue.

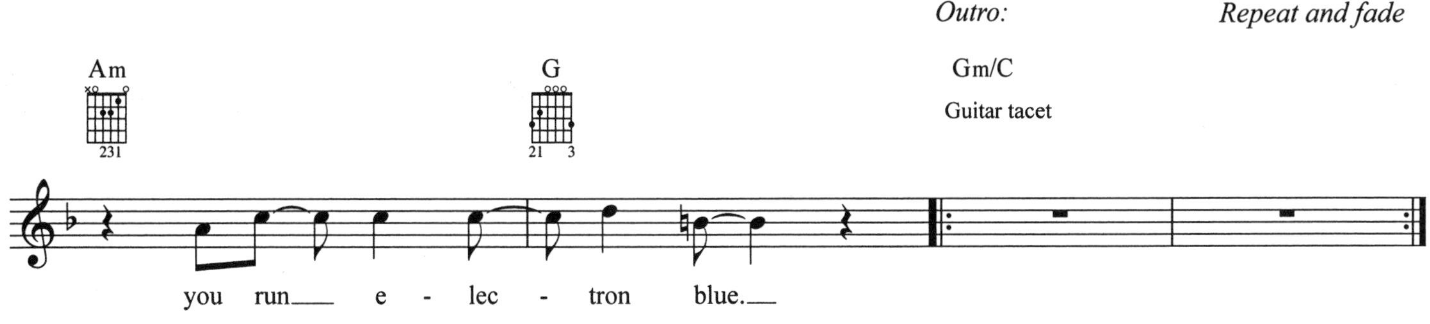

FINAL STRAW

Words and Music by
PETER BUCK, MIKE MILLS, MICHAEL STIPE

C Am7

lat - est tri - umph draws the fi - nal___ straw.
give - ness takes a back - seat to re - venge.
give - ness is the on - ly hope I___ hold.

Dm

Who___
There's a
And

Acous. Gtr. cont. rhy. simile

C Am7

died and lift - ed you up to per -
hurt down deep that has not been cor -
love, love will be my strong - est

Dm C

fec - tion? And what si - lenced me is writ -
rect - ed. There's a voice in me that says
wea - pon. I do be - lieve that I

Am7 Dm

ten in - to___ law. I
you will not___ win. And
am not a - lone. For this

*Elec. Gtr. 2nd & 3rd times only.

Dm
To Coda
1.
2.
Acous. Gtr. resume intro fig. simile
2. If
Now I
Bridge:
F
Dm
Acous. Gtr. cont. chorus fig. simile
don't be - lieve, and I nev - er did, that two wrongs make a right. If the
Elec. Gtr.
F
Dm
world were filled with the likes of you, then I'm put - ting up a fight, put - ting up a fight,

F
134211
Dm
231
Am
231
put-ting up a fight.
Make it right,
make it right.
Rhy. Fig. 1
C
32 1
Dm
231
D.S. 𝄋 al Coda
3. Now
end Rhy. Fig. 1
Coda
Chorus:
Dm
231
C
32 1
Dm
231
Acous. Gtr. cont. chorus fig. simile
Then I raise my voice up high - er and I
T
A
B

C
Dm
C
look you in the eye.
And I of - fer love with one con -
w/Rhy. Fig. 1 (Elec. Gtr.) 3 times, simile
Dm
Am
di - tion, with con - vic - tion, tell me
C
Dm
why, tell me why.
Tell me
Am
C
Dm
why, look me in the eye,
tell me why.
Am
C
Dm
Acous. Gtr.
Elec. Gtr.

HIGH SPEED TRAIN

Words and Music by
PETER BUCK, MIKE MILLS, MICHAEL STIPE

*Acous. Gtr. Verses 2 & 4 only; Verse 3 tacet.

C♯m
4fr.
13421
G
3fr.
134211
I told you I was a - fraid. Did
You've tak - en me by sur - prise. You've
I picked it my - self to - day. It
F
134211
E7
2 1
I real - ly want to try? You're hold - ing me to my claim.
mir-rored my best dis - guise and turned it back on me.
com - ple - ments your eyes. There's love at the end of line.
Chorus:
G
3fr.
134211
B
1333
Acous. Gtr. 1
Cont. rhy. simile
I jump on a high - speed train. I'll
Elec. Gtr. 1 2nd and 3rd time only; 1st time tacet
T
A
B

D
5fr.
1333
never look back again.
I flail like the antelope
F
134211
1.
E7
21
2.3.
E7
21
Acous. Gtr. 1
who
jumped from the building.
jumped from the building.
G
3fr.
134211
B
1333
Cont. rhy. simile
I jump on a high-speed train.
I'll

Guitar Solo:

E7 Am G Am

go an - y - where_ for you.___ Ooh.___

***Acous. Gtr. 1 & Elec. Gtr. 1**

Acous. Gtr. 2

*2 gtrs. arr. for 1 gtr.

D.S. 𝄋 al Coda
G
3fr.
134211
Am
231
G
3fr.
134211
F
134211
E7
2 1
Ooh.
Ooh.
Coda
E7
2 1
G
3fr.
134211
Acous. Gtr. 1
Cont. rhy. simile
go an - y - where for you.
And that's what I al - ways knew.
Elec. Gtr. 1

B
1333
D
5fr.
1333
I'd like to have hung the moon. I'd
F
134211
E7
2 1
wres-tle you for a spoon in - side your sleep-ing bag. Just us,
F
134211
E7
2 1
F
134211
no war, no hate, no past. It's real, I'm here, I'm yours,

E7
F
E7
2 1
134211
2 1
— I'm fast.— I'm long in the eye— I cry when I try,— I
T
A
B

Am
Acous. Gtr. 1
231
just want to fly,— just you— and I— to - geth - er.
T
A
B

Outro:

T
A
B

I WANTED TO BE WRONG

All gtrs. in Open E:
⑥ = E ③ = G♯
⑤ = B ② = B
④ = E ① = E

Words and Music by
PETER BUCK, MIKE MILLS, MICHAEL STIPE

E
E(9)/F♯
kicked my legs from un - der me___ and tried to take___ the wheel.___
Chorus 1:
A
B
B/F♯*
Cont. rhy. simile
I told you I want-ed to___ be wrong, but ev - 'ry - one___ is hum - ming a___
*F♯ played by bass gtr. only.
B/F♯
___ song that I don't un - der - stand.___
Resume intro. fig. simile
Verses 2 & 3:
Resume verse fig. simile
2. Now, I know that the sun___ has shined___ on my___
(3.) ro - de - o is stage - coach cir - cle, goat___
___ side of the street,___ the bas - ket of A - mer - i - ca,______ the wee-
___ rop - ers and clowns.___ A rum - ble in the third___ act; tie 'em up___
- vils and the wheat.___ The milk and hon-eyed con - gre - ga - tion,
___ and burn 'em down.___ We're armed to the teeth;___
5fr.
7fr.

E
E(9)/F♯
E
E(9)/F♯
scrubbed and ap-ple-cheeked, sa-lute A-pol-lo Thir-teen from the rat-
born a lit-tle breech. Blue-plate spe-cial an-a-lysts, cells
Chorus 2 & 3:
E
E(9)/F♯
A
5fr.
B
7fr.
tle jew'l-ry seats. My-thol-o-gy's se-duc-tive, and it turned
and S-U-Vs. We can't ap-proach the Al-lies 'cause they seem
A
B/F♯*
A
B/F♯*
a trick on me that I have just be-gun to un-der-stand.
a lit-tle peeved and speak a lan-guage we don't un-der-stand.
E
E(9)/F♯
E
E(9)/F♯
Resume intro. fig. simile
A
B
A
B/F♯*
I told you I want-ed to be wrong, but ev-'ry-one is hum-ming a
A
B/F♯*
E
E(9)/F♯
E
E(9)/F♯
Resume intro. fig. simile
song that I don't un-der-stand.

Bridge:
B
7fr.
111111
C♯m
8fr.
2134
D♯m
10fr.
2134
C♯m
B
C♯m
Acous. Gtr.
Cont. rhy. simile
Ooh, ooh, ooh, ooh, ooh, ooh. Ooh, ooh, ooh,
Elec. Gtr. 1
mf
*Elec. Gtr. 2
mf
*Elec. Gtr. 2 2nd time only.
D♯m
C♯m
B
C♯m
D♯m
C♯m
ooh, ooh, ooh, ooh. Ooh, ooh, ooh, ooh, ooh, ooh.

1.
2.
A
Asus(2)
G
Acous. Gtr.
3. The
Elec. Gtr. 2
Verse 4:
All gtrs. tacet 7 meas.
E
E(9)/F♯
Storm in - to the board - room of the con - quer - ing e - lite.
Did you rec - og - nize the mad - man who is shout - ing in the streets?
De - stroy the things that I don't un - der - stand.
De - stroy the things that I don't un - der - stand.
Resume intro. fig. simile
Acous. Gtr.

LEAVING NEW YORK

Words and Music by
PETER BUCK, MIKE MILLS, MICHAEL STIPE

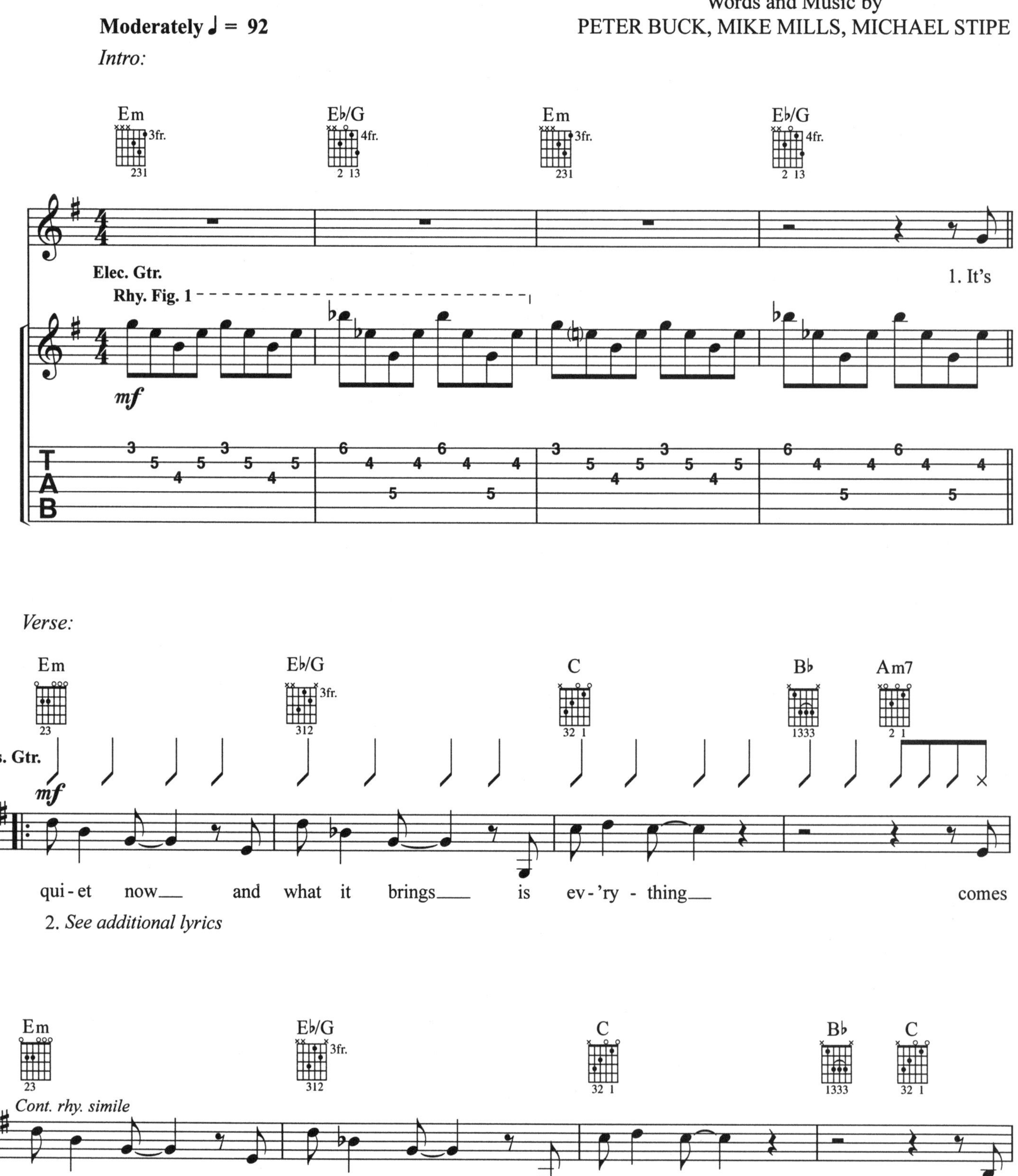

Em
Eb/G
3fr.
C
looked a - head, I'm sure I saw you there.
* Elec. Gtr.
*Elec. Gtr. 2nd time only.
Bb
Am7
Em
Eb/G
3fr.
You don't need me to tell you now that
C
Bb
C
noth - ing can com - pare.
Cont. in slashes

Chorus:
G
D
Dsus2
D
Elec. Gtr.
You might have laughed if I told you,
Vocal Fig. 1
(2nd & 3rd time) It's pull - ing me a -
(3rd time) nev - er, you nev - er, you told me for - ev - er.
C
Am
you might have hid - den a frown.
You
end Vocal Fig. 1
part,
change.
w/Vocal Fig. 1, 3 times, 2nd & 3rd times only
Cont. rhy. simile
might have suc - ceed - ed in chang - ing me.
I might have been turned a - round.
It's eas - ier to leave than to be left be - hind.

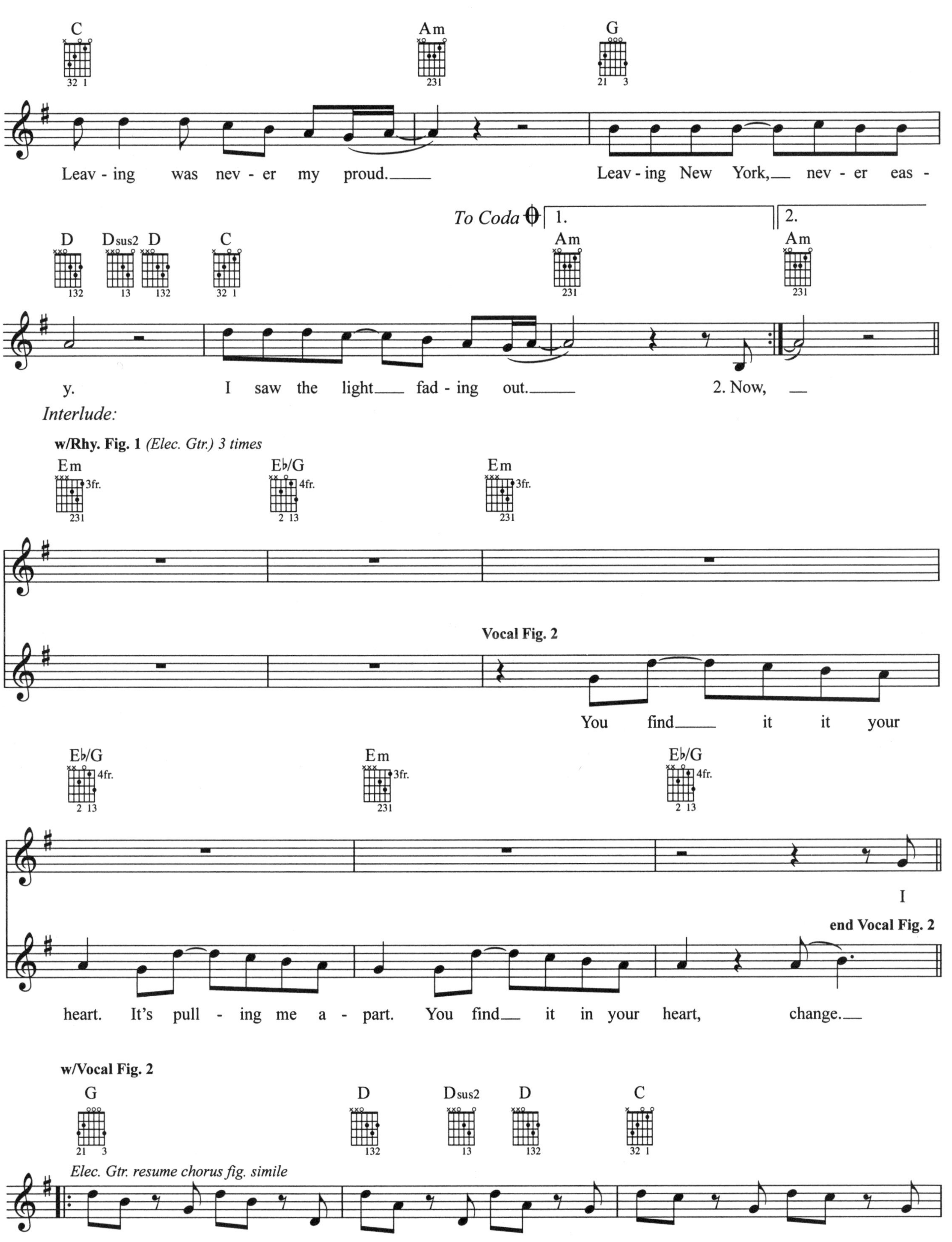
C
Am
G
Leav - ing was nev - er my proud.
Leav - ing New York, nev - er eas -
To Coda
1.
2.
D
Dsus2
D
C
Am
Am
y.
I saw the light fad - ing out.
2. Now,
Interlude:
w/Rhy. Fig. 1 (Elec. Gtr.) 3 times
Em
E♭/G
Em
Vocal Fig. 2
You find it it your
E♭/G
Em
E♭/G
I
end Vocal Fig. 2
heart. It's pull - ing me a - part. You find it in your heart, change.
w/Vocal Fig. 2
G
D
Dsus2
D
C
Elec. Gtr. resume chorus fig. simile
told you for - ev - er. I love you for - ev - er. I told you I love you, I

Verse 2:
Now, life is sweet and what it brings, I try to take.
But loneliness, it wears me out, it lies in wait.
And all not lost, still in my eye, the shadow of necklace across your thigh.
I might've lived my life in a dream, but I swear, this is real.
Memory fuses and shatters like glass, mercurial future, forget the past.
It's you, it's what I feel.
(To Chorus:)

MAKE IT ALL OKAY

w/Fill 1 (Elec. Gtr. 1) 1st time only
w/Fill 2 (Elec. Gtr. 2) 2nd & 3rd times only
Dm
Am/C
Gm7
C
big to ig - nore. Did-n't you, now? Did-n't you? So, you
make it all o - kay. Did-n't you, now? Did-n't you? So our
help me through my day. Did-n't you, now? Did-n't you? But
Chorus:
Am
D
worked out your ex - cus - es, turned a - way and shut the door. The
past has been re - writ - ten and you threw a - way the pen. You'd
Je - sus loves me fine, but his
Elec. Gtr. 1
Am
D
world's too vast for us now and you want - ed to ex - plore. It's a
said that I was use - less, but now you'll take me in a - gain. Well,
words fall flat this time. It's a

Em
C
long, long, long road and I
Je - sus loves me fine, and your
long, long, long road and I
Elec. Gtr. 2
T
A
B
Em
C
don't know which way to go. If you
words fall flat this time. Was it
don't know which way to go. If you
1.
Em
Dm
C
of - fered me your hand a - gain, I'd have to walk a - way.
my i - mag - i - na - tion, or
of - fered me your world did you

2.
3.
B♭
B♭(♯11)
Dm
C
Em
Acous. Gtr.
2. When I did I hear you say, "We don't
have a prayer be - tween us ?"
think I'd real - ly stay? If you
of - fered me the heav - ens, I would
have to turn a - way. Was it

Em
Dm
C
my i - mag - i - na - tion or did I hear you say, "We don't
Bb
Bb(#11)
Bb
Bb(#11)
have a prayer be - tween us?" Did - n't you, now? Did - n't
Bb
Bb(#11)
F
rit.
Acous. Gtr.
you, now? Did - n't you?
rit.

THE ASCENT OF MAN

Words and Music by
PETER BUCK, MIKE MILLS, MICHAEL STIPE

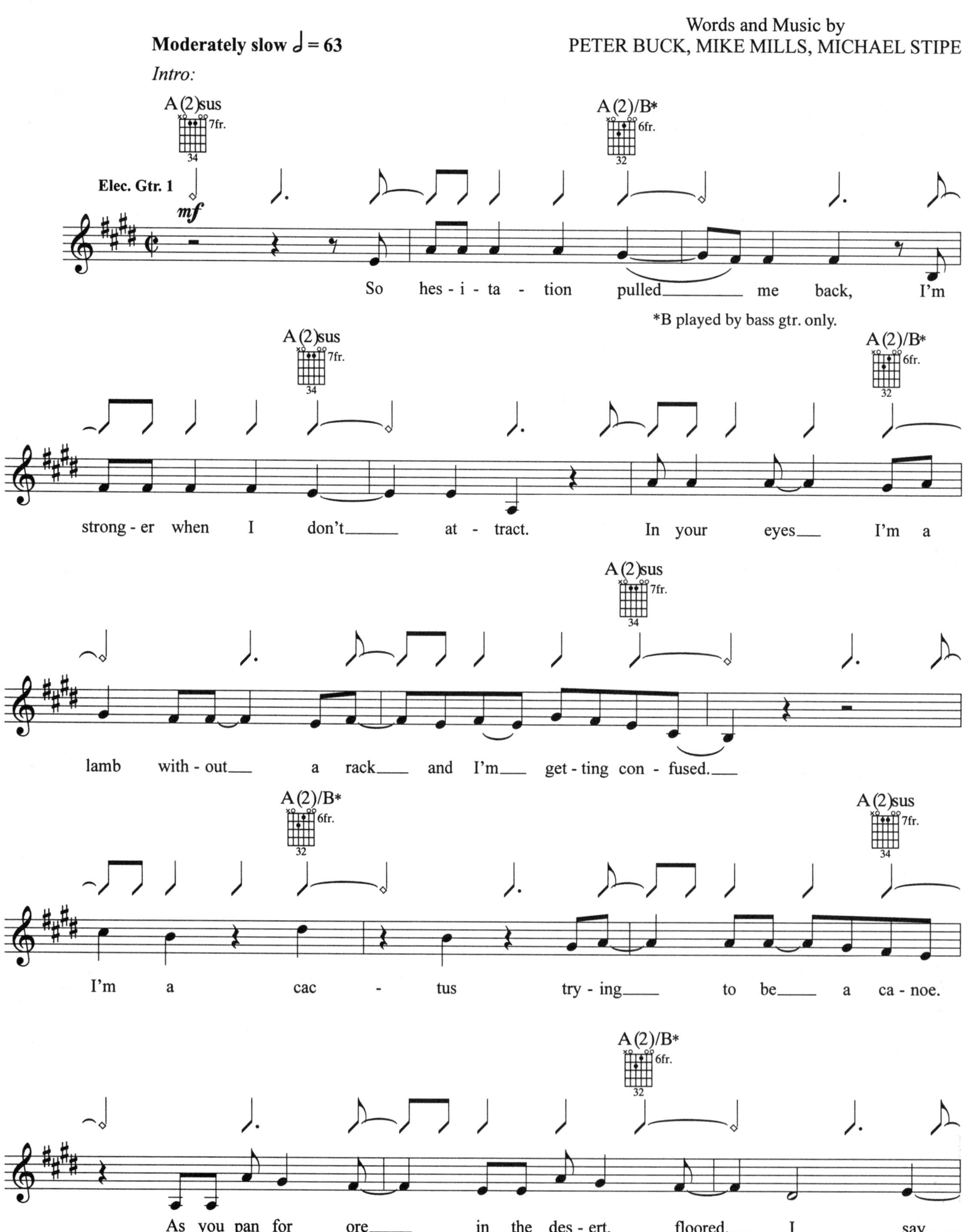

Verse:
B
7fr.
134211
to you.
1. That I could nev - er i - mag - ine a place
2.3. See additional lyrics
Elec. Gtr. 2
mf
**Sitar (arr. for gtr.)
mf
*Elec. Gtr. 3
D♯m7
6fr.
13121
G♯m7
4fr.
131111
so beau - ti - ful I could nev - er steal your

Chorus:
F♯m7
B7
E
B5
C♯m
4fr.
gold a - way. Yeah, yeah, yeah, yeah, yeah,
Elec. Gtr. 3
hold
*Sitar
*Third time only.
E
B5
Elec. Gtr. 3 cont. simile
yeah. Yeah, yeah. yeah, yeah, yeah,
(I try to walk like a big wham bam.
hold

To Coda
C♯m
4fr.
13421
E
231
B5
133
yeah.
Yeah, yeah, yeah, yeah, yeah,
I came a-cross like a bat-ter-ing ram,
I try to float like a tel-e-gram, Sam, I'm
C♯m
4fr.
13421
F♯
134211
F♯sus
3411
F♯
134211
yeah.
try - ing to di-vine you.)
Elec. Gtr. 3
1.
E
231
2.
hold

Interlude:
Bm
A6
A(2)
6fr.
Acous. Gtr.
mf
Elec. Gtr. 2
D.S. 𝄋 al Coda
D7
D9sus
D7
D9sus
D7
5fr.
G6
G
G6
G
F♯
E
Coda
C♯m
4fr.
E
B5
yeah.
Yeah, yeah, yeah, yeah, yeah,
Sitar
try - ing to di-vine you.)
(I try to walk like a big wham bam,

C♯m
4fr.
13421
E
231
B5
133
yeah.
Yeah, yeah, yeah, yeah, yeah,
I came a-cross like a bat-ter-ing ram,
I try to float like a tel-e-gram, Sam, I'm
T
A
B
C♯m
4fr.
13421
E
231
B5
133
C♯5
4fr.
133
yeah.
try - ing to di - vine you.)
Elec. Gtr. 3
Sitar

Verse 2:
My book is called, "The Ascent of Man."
I marked your chapter with a catamaran.
The accent's off.
But I am what I am.
(To Chorus:)

Verse 3:
I looked for you. It's my last grandstand.
A motorscootered goat-legged pan
Figure-eighting in quicksand.
(To Chorus:)

THE OUTSIDERS

G
D/F♯*
Em
C
D
pro-mis-ing vol-can-ic change of plot. Where will this lead us? I'm scared of the storm. The
*F♯ played by bass gtr. only.
Em
D
Em
Verse 2:
D
Em
out-sid-ers are gath-er-ing, a new day is born. I tried to tell you I am not a-fraid.
Elec. Gtr. 2
Elec. Gtr. 2 cont. simile
D
Em
D
You looked up and saw it all a-cross my face. So am I with you or
Em
D
Em
am I a-gainst? I don't think it's that eas-y, we're lost in re-gret. Now, I'm

D
G
A
try - ing to re - mem - ber the feel - ing when the mu - sic stopped,
Em
D
Em
D
when you told me what you knew.
Lost in the mo-ment the
G
A
Em
D
day that the mu - sic stopped.
And I do re - mem - ber you.
Chorus:
Em
C
D
Elec. Gtr. 2 resume chorus fig. simile
Draw-ing pat-terns with the cork on the ta - ble cloth,
Elec. Gtr. 1
Elec. Gtr. 3
mf
G
D/F♯*
Em
C
pro-mis-ing vol - can - ic change of plot.
Where does this leave us? I'm

D
Em
D
Em
scared of the storm.
The out-sid-ers are gath-er-ing, a new day is born.
C
D
G
D/F#*
Draw-ing pat-terns with the cork on the ta-ble cloth,
pro-mis-ing vol-can-ic change
Em
C
D
of thought.
Where does this leave us? I'm scared of the storm.
The
Elec. Gtr. 3 tacet
TAB

Rap:
A man walks away when every muscle says to stay.
How many yesterdays? They each weigh heavy.
Who says what changes may come?
Who says what we call home?
I know you see right through me, my luminescence fades.
The dusk provides an antidote, I am not afraid.
I've been a million times in my mind
And this is really just a technicality, frailty, reality.

Uh, it's time to breathe, time to believe.
Let it go and run towards the sea.
They don't teach that, they don't know what you mean.
They don't understand, they don't know what you mean.
They don't get it, I wanna scream.
I want to breathe again, I want to dream
I want to float a quote from Martin Luther King.
I am not afraid, I am not afraid, I am not afraid... etc.

WANDERLUST

Words and Music by
PETER BUCK, MIKE MILLS, MICHAEL STIPE

Verse:
Am
F
C
Cont. rhy. simile
1. Looks like I pulled a fast one. Looks like I went to town.
2. I had to grab a suit - case. I had to change my clothes.
E7
Am
F
Looks like the world re - volves a - round me.
I had to run the show - er hot
C
D
Am
Looks like it's fall - ing down.
un - til the wa - ter froze.
I thought I'd kicked the trac - es.
I brushed a - gainst con - fu - sion.
* Elec. Gtr. 2
*Elec. Gtr. 2 tacet 1st 7 meas., 1st time only.
F
C
E7
I thought the wheels would spin.
I want - ed time to grow.

Am
231
F
134211
C
32 1
I thought I'd jumped the fence and bolt - ed. Looks like I'm back a - gain.
I want the sticks and stones not to throw me. Get back to what I
D
132
know.
Chorus:
G
21 3
Bm
13421
Acous. Gtr. resume intro fig. simile
I got my sig - nals crossed.
Elec. Gtr. 1
A
111
G
21 3
Bm
13421
A
111
It's o - ver - whelm - ing be - cause

G
Bm
A
B7
I'm all a-lone and I can't get back, get back with my wan-der - lust.
1.
2.
Bridge:
F♯
Acous. Gtr. resume verse fig. simile
I'm search-ing for a great-
Bm
F♯
Bm
F♯
- ness. I smear it on my face. I want to bathe in grape;
TAB

Bm
Bm(maj7)
Bm7
Bm6
G
E7
— must swim — the length — of the Milk - y Way. — I want it to be
bril-liant. I want it to be sweet. I want to kiss the as - tro-nauts when they sa - lute to
Chorus:
A
Acous. Gtr. resume intro fig. simile
me, me, me, me. I got my sig - nals crossed. —

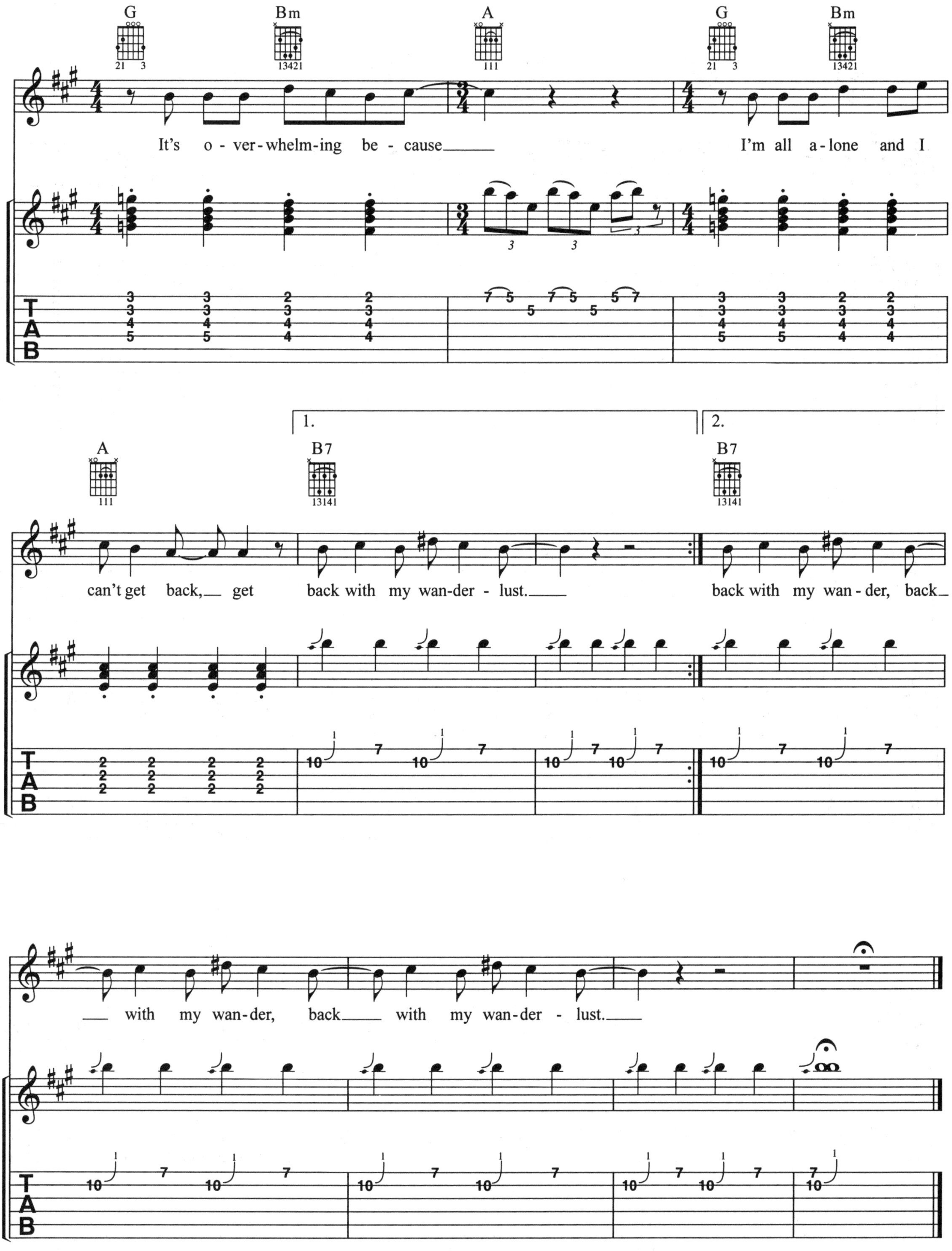

G Bm A G Bm

It's o-ver-whelm-ing be-cause_____ I'm all a-lone and I

TAB

1. 2.

A B7 B7

can't get back,__ get back with my wan-der-lust.____ back with my wan-der, back_

TAB

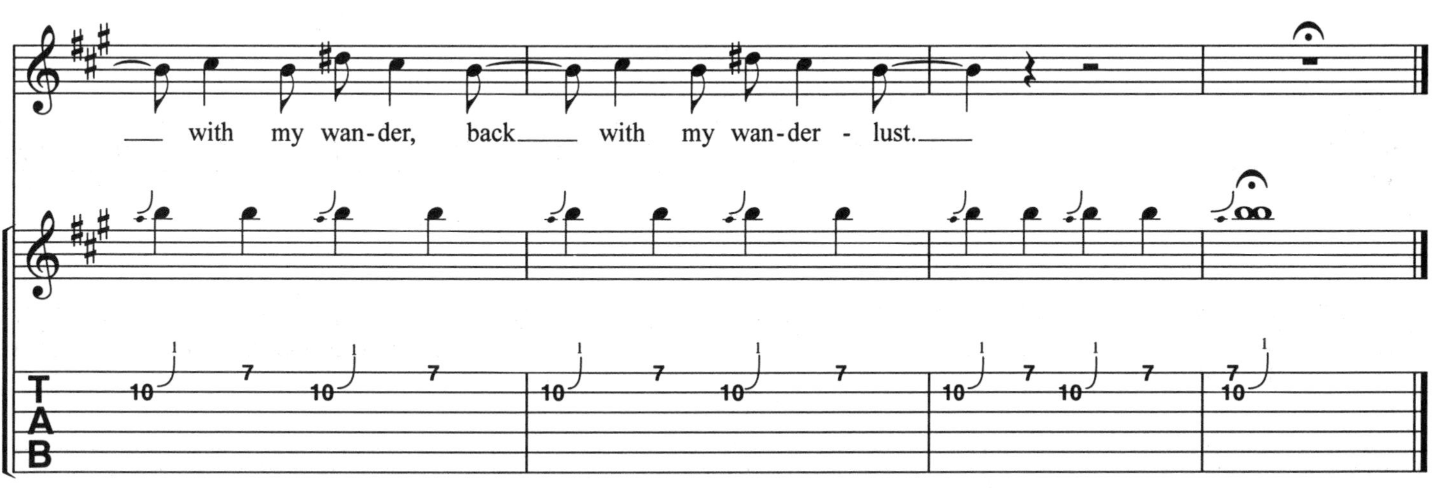

THE WORST JOKE EVER

Words and Music by
PETER BUCK, MIKE MILLS, MICHAEL STIPE

The Worst Joke Ever - 7 - 1
PGM0426

Am
Em
Some things don't hold up o-ver the course of a life - time.
Am
Am
Oh.
When's the first time you heard that one,
Em
F
Em
Acous. Gtr.
Nine-teen Fif-ty - Four?
Get to the punch line.
Fall to the floor.
Chorus:
G
3fr.
Dm
5fr.
Rhy. Fig. 1
Give me a min - ute and I'll tell you the set - up for the
Rhy. Fig. 1A
Elec. Gtr. 1
mf
hold throughout
Rhy. Fig. 1B
Elec. Gtr. 2
mf

Cm
1342
B♭
1333
F
134211
worst joke ever, I never.
T
A
B
G
3fr.
134211
Dm
5fr.
1342
I'll tell you my ver-sion of the great-est life sto-ry.

w/Fill 1 (Elec. Gtr. 3)
To Coda
Cm
1342
B♭
1333
F
134211
end Rhy. Fig. 1
Cont. in notation
Don't bore me.
end Rhy. Fig. 1A
end Rhy. Fig. 1B
Verse 2:
Am
231
Em
3
Am
231
Now I am float-ing, I feel re - leased. The moor-ings have been dropped, the
Acous. Gtr.
hold throughout
Fill 1
Elec. Gtr. 3
mf

Em
Am
Em
weight's un - leashed.
Ev-'ry - thing is crys - tal - line,
sim - ple and free.
F
Em
Oh.
The
Cont. in slashes
Am
Em
Acous. Gtr.
Cont. rhy. simile
crime of good men who can't wres - tle with change or are too a - fraid to face
Am
Em
Am
this life's mis - judged un - knowns.
You're not hurt - ing an - y - bod - y
D.S. 𝄋 al Coda
Em
F
Em
el - se's chanc - es.
But you're dis - fig - ur - ing your own.

Coda
w/Rhy. Figs. 1 (Acous. Gtr.), 1A (Elec. Gtr. 1), & 1B (Elec. Gtr. 2)
simile
B♭
F
G
3fr.
I never.
Give me a min-ute and I'll
Dm
5fr.
Cm
B♭
F
tell you the set-up,
oh.
w/Fill 1 (Elec. Gtr. 3)
G
3fr.
Dm
5fr.
Cm
B♭
F
You see, there's this feel-ing that I've heard this one be-fore.

Outro:
G
3fr.
134211
Em
23
Acous. Gtr.
Elec. Gtr. 1
Cont. in notation
Acous. Gtr. & Elec. Gtr. 1
hold throughout
Elec. Gtr. 2
Em7
4
Em6
3
Em7
4
Em
23

GUITAR TAB GLOSSARY **

TABLATURE EXPLANATION

READING TABLATURE: Tablature illustrates the six strings of the guitar. Notes and chords are indicated by the placement of fret numbers on a given string(s).

BENDING NOTES

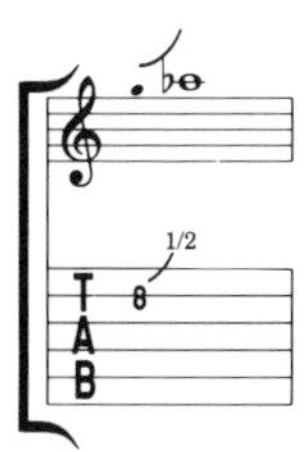

HALF STEP: Play the note and bend string one half step.*

WHOLE STEP: Play the note and bend string one whole step.

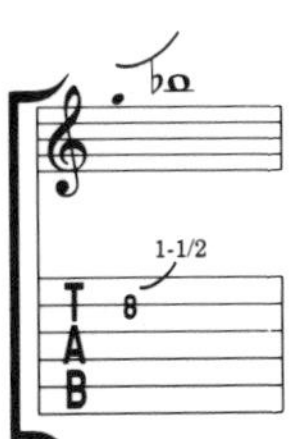

WHOLE STEP AND A HALF: Play the note and bend string a whole step and a half.

SLIGHT BEND (Microtone): Play the note and bend string slightly to the equivalent of half a fret.

*A half step is the smallest interval in Western music; it is equal to one fret. A whole step equals two frets.

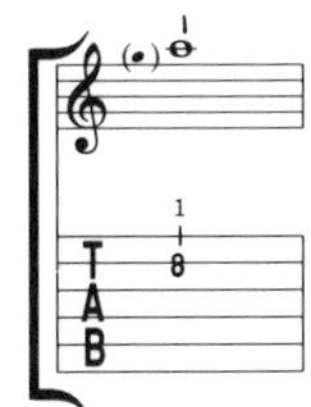

PREBEND (Ghost Bend): Bend to the specified note, before the string is picked.

PREBEND AND RELEASE: Bend the string, play it, then release to the original note.

REVERSE BEND: Play the already-bent string, then immediately drop it down to the fretted note.

BEND AND RELEASE: Play the note and gradually bend to the next pitch, then release to the original note. Only the first note is attacked.

UNISON BEND: Play both notes and immediately bend the lower note to the same pitch as the higher note.

DOUBLE NOTE BEND: Play both notes and immediately bend both strings simultaneously.

BENDS INVOLVING MORE THAN ONE STRING: Play the note and bend string while playing an additional note (or notes) on another string(s). Upon release, relieve pressure from additional note(s), causing original note to sound alone.

BENDS INVOLVING STATIONARY NOTES: Play notes and bend lower pitch, then hold until release begins (indicated at the point where line becomes solid).

TREMOLO BAR

SPECIFIED INTERVAL: The pitch of a note or chord is lowered to a specified interval and then may or may not return to the original pitch. The activity of the tremolo bar is graphically represented by peaks and valleys.

UN-SPECIFIED INTERVAL: The pitch of a note or a chord is lowered to an unspecified interval.

HARMONICS

NATURAL HARMONIC: A finger of the fret hand lightly touches the note or notes indicated in the tab and is played by the pick hand.

ARTIFICIAL HARMONIC: The first tab number is fretted, then the pick hand produces the harmonic by using a finger to lightly touch the same string at the second tab number (in parenthesis) and is then picked by another finger.

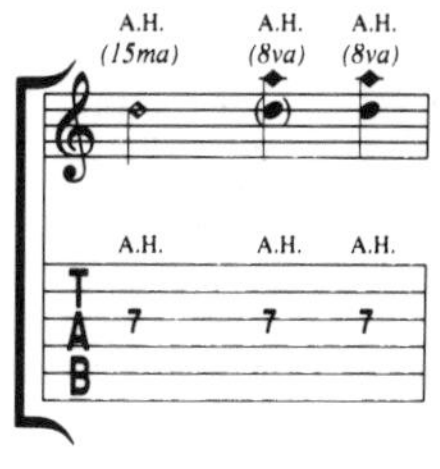

ARTIFICIAL "PINCH" HAR-MONIC: A note is fretted as indicated by the tab, then the pick hand produces the harmonic by squeezing the pick firmly while using the tip of the index finger in the pick attack. If parenthesis are found around the fretted note, it does not sound. No parenthesis means both the fretted note and A.H. are heard simultaneously.

**By Kenn Chipkin and Aaron Stang

RHYTHM SLASHES

STRUM INDICATIONS: Strum with indicated rhythm.

The chord voicings are found on the first page of the transcription underneath the song title.

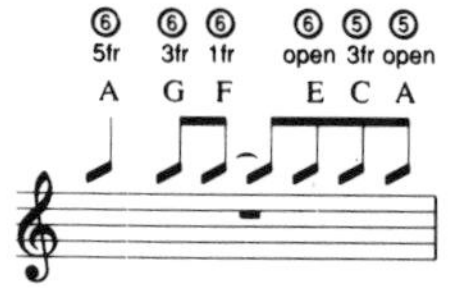

INDICATING SINGLE NOTES USING RHYTHM SLASHES: Very often single notes are incorporated into a rhythm part. The note name is indicated above the rhythm slash with a fret number and a string indication.

ARTICULATIONS

HAMMER ON: Play lower note, then "hammer on" to higher note with another finger. Only the first note is attacked.

LEFT HAND HAMMER: Hammer on the first note played on each string with the left hand.

PULL OFF: Play higher note, then "pull off" to lower note with another finger. Only the first note is attacked.

FRETBOARD TAPPING: "Tap" onto the note indicated by + with a finger of the pick hand, then pull off to the following note held by the fret hand.

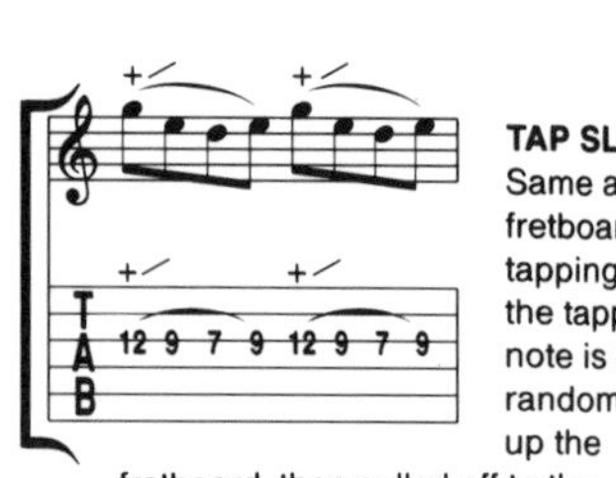

TAP SLIDE: Same as fretboard tapping, but the tapped note is slid randomly up the fretboard, then pulled off to the following note.

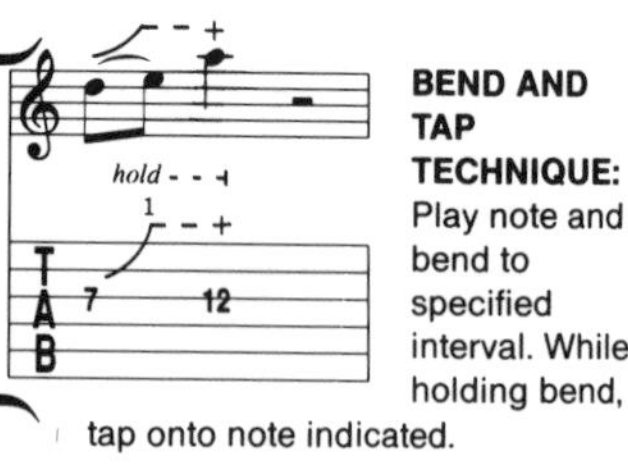

BEND AND TAP TECHNIQUE: Play note and bend to specified interval. While holding bend, tap onto note indicated.

LEGATO SLIDE: Play note and slide to the following note. (Only first note is attacked).

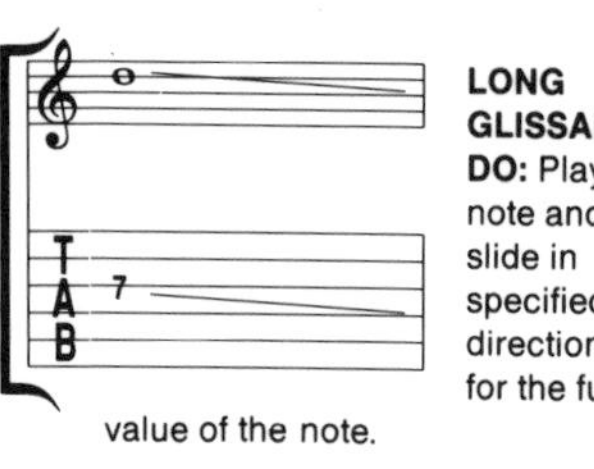

LONG GLISSANDO: Play note and slide in specified direction for the full value of the note.

SHORT GLISSANDO: Play note for its full value and slide in specified direction at the last possible moment.

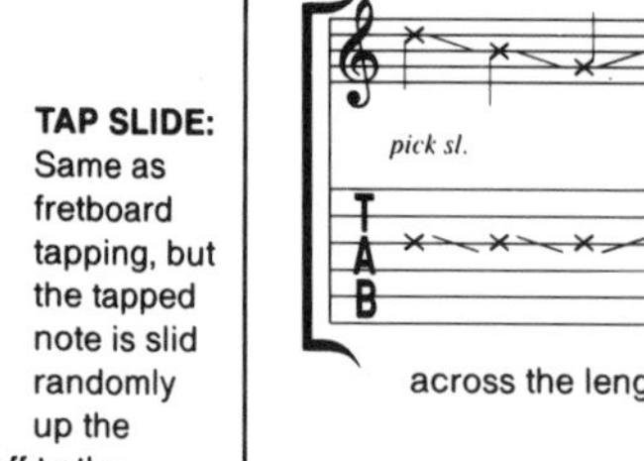

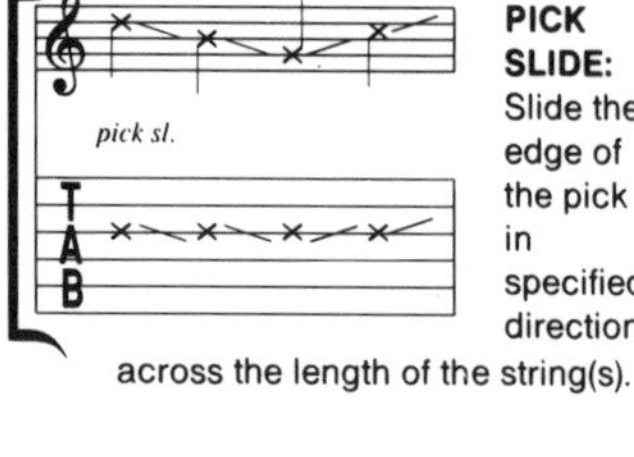

PICK SLIDE: Slide the edge of the pick in specified direction across the length of the string(s).

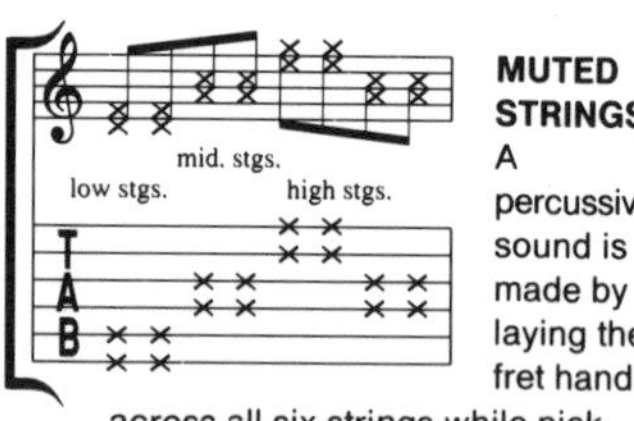

MUTED STRINGS: A percussive sound is made by laying the fret hand across all six strings while pick hand strikes specified area (low, mid, high strings).

PALM MUTE: The note or notes are muted by the palm of the pick hand by lightly touching the string(s) near the bridge.

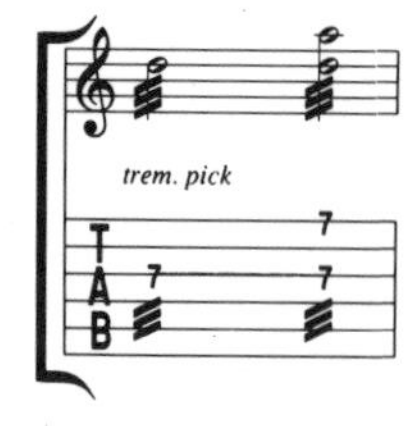

TREMOLO PICKING: The note or notes are picked as fast as possible.

TRILL: Hammer on and pull off consecutively and as fast as possible between the original note and the grace note.

ACCENT: Notes or chords are to be played with added emphasis.

STACCATO (Detached Notes): Notes or chords are to be played roughly half their actual value and with separation.

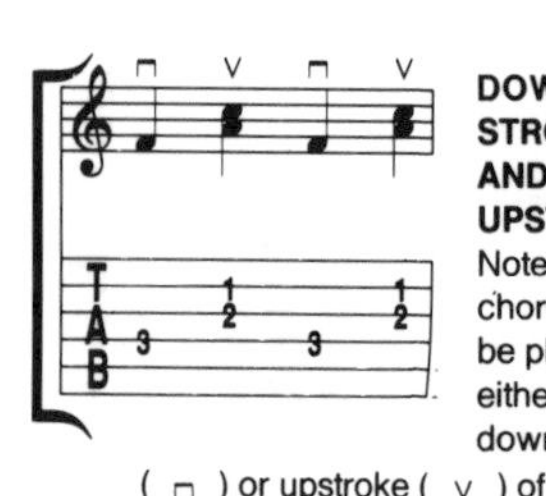

DOWN STROKES AND UPSTROKES: Notes or chords are to be played with either a downstroke (⊓) or upstroke (v) of the pick.

VIBRATO: The pitch of a note is varied by a rapid shaking of the fret hand finger, wrist, and forearm.